Reflections for the Effective Nonprofit Volunteer

A volume of the Effective Philanthropy and
Fund Raising series.

Reflections for the Effective Nonprofit Volunteer

Quotes, axioms and observations to help you serve our important institutions

Jim Norvell

Writers Club Press

San Jose   New York   Lincoln   Shanghai

Reflections for the Effective Nonprofit Volunteer
Quotes, axioms and observations to
help you serve our important institutions

Writers Club Press
an imprint of iUniverse, Inc.

For information address:
iUniverse, Inc.
5220 S. 16th St., Suite 200
Lincoln, NE 68512
www.iuniverse.com

Artistic license was exercised with the quotes borrowed from an illustrious array
of thoughtful people. Insertion of their observations in juxtaposition to my
own was based on their unique similarity, often taken out of context. Those
who are still around to do so are free to do the same with mine.

ISBN: 0-595-20884-3

Printed in the United States of America

Inspiration

During my years as a fundraiser, I have worked with extraordinary volunteers at every nonprofit level. From multimillionaire businesspeople to homemakers, all have had a drive to be useful to their communities and true to their beliefs. This benevolence to not only friends but strangers, too, is a particularly human trait. It is impossible not to be moved by generosity, whether it is an enormous donation of money or a gift of precious time. The predisposition to service and charity is almost genetically coded. Only a rare few are left out of this admirable gene pool, and it diminishes their lives.

The most inspirational volunteer I ever met was Harriette Witmer, a fine arts graduate of UCLA and proud wife of a Cal Tech engineer who had built a small chemical company in southern California. She was rearing two teenage sons in 1972 when an Air Canada crash killed 109 people, including her husband.

 Junior League was over for Harriette and Deepwater Chemical was in deep water. Finding a resolve previously dormant, she assumed leadership of the company. Burying her grief in activity, she solidified the finances, found new customers and built a solid reputation for management acumen. Her success and demeanor carried her to the national chairmanship (her preferred terminology) of her industry's trade association, the first woman to hold the post. Not bad for an Arts major housewife.

Always a volunteer, she could not refuse Newport Harbor Art Museum's board invitation. In the ensuing years, she became president. Proud of her alma mater, she was an active alumna for it, too. She had a full plate.

Then South Coast Repertory (SCR) had ambitions to build a theatre. A gift of land was secured, but no one was willing to chair the long-shot fund-raising campaign. The SCR board reached out to Harriette, relying on her strong reputation as a leader at the museum. Yielding to the petition of friends, she assumed chairmanship of the building campaign, the largest attempted in Orange County at that time. She enlisted a team of solicitors with far greater wealth and public profile than she and drove the campaign to a successful conclusion.

Now, twenty-five years after, SCR enjoys national renown and Orange County has a world-class Performing Arts Center. A vibrant cultural support base boasts the most prominent business and social leaders of Southern California. That legacy is a testament to the philanthropy of thousands and, notably, the Segerstrom family, but its genesis was the moment in 1976 when one woman, Harriette Witmer, volunteered to chair SCR's campaign.

Jim Norvell

For my mother, Myrtle Fischer, who is always there for family, friends, her church and me.

You must do the thing you think you cannot do.

Eleanor Roosevelt

Quotes, axioms and observations to help you expand our important institutions

This book was compiled as a resource for nonprofit volunteers. It contains some of the key guidelines I have found to be useful in serving nonprofit organizations. Finally, I wrote it because I like quotes and have found that many of you share that enjoyment.

The inequities of life demand philanthropy.

We must build a new world, a far better world—one in which the eternal dignity of man is respected.

Harry S. Truman

Social consciousness is the first step in a philanthropic solution.

We must have the press of the crowd to draw virtue from us.

Angelo Patri

If the gift does not affect the donor's life, it is merely a handout—not philanthropy.

Do not be conformed to this world, but be transformed.

Romans 12:2 (NRSV)

Philanthropy is created by the same drives that fuel competition.

All of our dreams can come true—if we have the courage to pursue them.

Walt Disney

Most philanthropy is based on emotion.

Emotion has taught mankind to reason.

Marquis de Vauvenargues

Philanthropy is the socialism of democracy.

Whoever has two coats must share with anyone who has none; and whoever has food must do likewise.

Luke 3

The more social freedom we experience, the greater our need for philanthropy.

I believe we are here on planet earth to live, grow up, and do what we can to make this world a better place for all people to enjoy freedom.

Rosa Parks

Philanthropy is second only to the vote in embodying democracy.

Money spent on ourselves may be a millstone around the neck; spent on others it may give us wings like eagles.

Roswell Dwight Hitchcock

Philanthropy alone cannot bridge all social inequities; but, with government as an ally and enabler, it can minimize them.

Giving away a fortune is taking Christianity too far.

Charlotte Bingham

The quality of life in the United States would be unexceptional without philanthropy.

If there is one word that describes our form of society in America, it may be the word—voluntary.

Lyndon Baines Johnson

Philanthropy is a quid pro quo transaction.

As the purse is emptied, the heart is filled.

Victor Hugo

Altruism is more likely to appear as instinctual heroism rather than charity.

There are two perfectly good men; one dead and the other yet unborn.

Chinese proverb

A philanthropic transaction is a valuation and an exchange.

Decide what you want, decide what you are willing to exchange for it. Establish your priorities and go to work.

H. L. Hunt

Self interest regulates all transactions, philanthropy included.

A man does not have to be an angel to be a saint.

Albert Schweitzer

The philanthropic exchange is not always apparent.

A bone to the dog is not charity. Charity is the bone shared with the dog, when you are just as hungry as the dog.

Jack London

Negotiation is common in major philanthropic transactions.

Let every eye negotiate for itself
And trust no agent.

William Shakespeare

Worthiness is not inherent in a nonprofit organization; it is granted by stakeholders.

If I say it, they can doubt me; if they say it, it's true.

Tom Hopkins

Altruism is highly overrated.

Every major horror in history was committed in the name of an altruistic motive.

Ayn Rand

The Philanthropic Sector is a response to life's inequities and the need to serve.

Life has no meaning except in terms of responsibility.

Reinhold Niebuhr

Social consciousness is at the root of philanthropy.

We will have to repent in this generation not merely for the vitriolic words and actions of bad people, but for the appalling silence of the good people.

Martin Luther King, Jr.

Philanthropic acts stem from resonance between the needs of others and personal value systems.

Many organizations are very clear about the needs they would like to serve, but they don't understand these needs from the perspective of the customers.

Philip Kotler

Philanthropy is a gift on one side and a promise on the other.

*A mind conscious of integrity scorns to say
more than it means to perform.*

Robert Burns

Everyone has needs that philanthropy meets.

Trouble is a part of your life, and if you don't share it, you don't give the person who loves you enough chance to love you enough.

Dinah Shore

Nonprofit privilege and huge revenue
stream make philanthropy an inviting
target for government control.

Those who worry about the motives of the charitable bolster their own political attitudes or comfort themselves with their own miserliness.

Benedict Nightingale

Philanthropy is too often marketed only through fund raising.

I get fifteen or twenty letters a day for everything from Yugoslavian dog illnesses to marathon diseases. It numbs you. So you write off a check for twenty dollars to a charity to absolve yourself of guilt.

Anjelica Huston

Philanthropy is both a behavior and an ideal.

Be not merely good; be good for something.

Henry David Thoreau

We have an inherent need to reinforce personal values.

The poor don't know that their function in life is to exercise our generosity.

Jean Paul Sartre

Need is the perception of deficiency and the opportunity to approach fulfillment.

A poor person who is unhappy is in a better position than a rich person who is unhappy. Because the poor person has hope. He thinks money would help.

Jean Kerr

Everything is a value judgment.

Values are the lens through which self sees the world.

Tom Reynolds

Personal values are not static, but changes
are few and far between.

All change is not growth; all movement is not forward.

Ellen Glasgow

People differentiate nonprofits by evaluating them against their personal value systems.

Caring is personal. It is rooted in an individual's own set of values, concerns and aspirations.

Peter M. Senge

Instinctual response and the conditioning of experience shape human behavior.

Men are wise in proportion, not to their experience, but to their capacity for experience.

George Bernard Shaw

Personal needs are an effort to shape reality.

Reality is something that you rise above.

Liza Minnelli

Life is defined by the drive to fulfill personal needs.

The significance of man is not what he attains but rather what he hopes to attain.

Kahlil Gibran

Values evolve to regulate needs.

It's not hard to make decisions when you know what your values are.

Roy Disney

Individual values regulate decision-making processes.

Why does a man act as he does? What would be required for a man to act differently? The key to motivation lies in the realm of values.

Nathaniel Brandon

Choices reflect and reinforce deeply-held values.

We don't see things as they are, we see them as we are.

Anaïs Nin

We are uniquely defined by the way we express our values.

A man is literally what he thinks.

James Allen

Jim Norvell

The perceived consequences of behavior are balanced against personal goals.

You can do anything in the world if you are prepared to take the consequences.

W. Somerset Maugham

Understanding group values increases likelihood of developing linkages.

Public opinion is a thermometer a monarch should constantly consult.

Napoleon I

We reveal our values when we tell others
what is important to us.

Friends are my heart and my ears.

Michael Jordan

Nonprofits should periodically research constituent values to understand the "mind of the market."

Grace is given of God, but knowledge is bought in the market.

Arthur Hugh Clough

Gifts reflect the donor's needs.

Nobody has ever measured, even poets, how much the heart can hold.

Zelda Fitzgerald

Donors satisfy value-driven needs when they provide philanthropic support.

I have found that the best way to give advice to your children is to find out what they want and then advise them to do it.

Harry S. Truman

Donors have rights that organizations should look upon as obligations.

There's no such thing as a free lunch.

Milton Friedman

Situational ethics aren't ethical.

I think its better to come in second than to be impeached.

George McGovern

Character is the expression ethical standards.

In matters of style, swim with the current; in matters of principle, stand like a rock.

Thomas Jefferson

Commitment to ethical standards defines organizations and people.

If ever I said, in grief or pride, I tired of honest things, I lied.

Edna St.Vincent Millay

Influential leaders shape the organizational culture.

The manager administers, the leader innovates. The manager maintains, the leader develops. The manager relies on systems, the leader relies on people. The manager does things right, the leader does the right things.

Forbes Magazine

Nonprofits must abide by ethical standards in a much more public way than private sector organizations.

Many people like to believe charities as dishonest as they are supposedly mismanaged. They actually prefer them that way, because it means that they do not have to feel guilty about their own lack of generosity.

Benedict Nightingale

Fund raising's fiduciary implications demand specific ethical standards of the highest magnitude.

The knights had to vow poverty, chastity, and obedience. They only kept the last vow.

Gen. George S. Patton, Jr.

Ethics are a contract between the organization and its constituents.

I only know that what is moral is what you feel good after and what is immoral is what you feel bad after.

Ernest Hemingway

Ethical conduct is influenced, but not guaranteed by standards.

*My best friend is the one who brings out
the best in me.*

Henry Ford

The highest ideals demand the highest
standards of conduct.

The ultimate test for us of what truth means is the conduct it dictates or inspires.

William James

The most influential traits are those that exhibit sensitivity to others.

Quick sensitiveness is inseparable from a ready understanding.

Joseph Addison

Personal attributes generate more influence than authority.

I learned that a great leader is a man who has the ability to get other people to do what they don't want to do and like it.

Harry S. Truman

Nonprofits compete with vacations, second homes, baubles and hobbies.

To vie is not to rival.

Benjamin Disraeli

No one solicits more effectively than a social equal of the prospect.

The pressure of social influence about us is enormous, and no single arm can resist it.

Felix Alder

The more impersonal the solicitation the less likely significant support.

I have known people to stop and buy an apple on the corner and then walk away as if they have solved the whole unemployment problem.

Heywood Broun

Donor prospects respond to example, peer challenge and incentive.

It is not fair to ask of others what you are not willing to do yourself.

Eleanor Roosevelt

Commitment to shared values shapes the organizational culture.

If you don't have a shared value system, you don't have an inner source of security.

Stephen R. Covey

The ideal nonprofit is professionally managed and volunteer led.

The test of a first-rate intelligence is the ability to hold two opposed ideas in the mind at the same time, and still retain the ability to function.

F. Scott Fitzgerald

Fund raising is best managed by experienced professionals and done by respected volunteers.

When the professional's fund-raising knowledge and management skills are combined with the volunteer's influence, the result is success.

James Gregory Lord

Board members provide leadership best through planning, stewardship and evaluation.

As for him who voluntarily performs a good work, verily God is grateful and knowing.

The Koran, Ch. 2

No one solicits as effectively as a committed volunteer, only the chief staff officer is a close second.

Ya gotta do what ya gotta do.

Sylvester Stallone (as Rocky Balboa in "Rocky IV")

No paid employee carries the credibility of a committed volunteer.

You give little when you give of your possessions. It is when you give of yourself that you truly gain.

Kahlil Gibran

Someone has to show the way for others.

Do it big or stay in bed.

Opera promoter Larry Kelly

Volunteers run from conflict.

Tranquility will roof a house, but discord can wear away the foundation of a city.

Ernest Bramah

About the Author

James R. (Jim) Norvell

Jim is a second-generation fundraiser who began his career immediately after graduating from Southern Illinois University–Edwardsville. He served in annual fund positions at Monticello College, the Foundation for Independent Colleges of Pennsylvania and Washington University before joining G. A. Brakeley & Co., Inc., Los Angeles, as a capital fundraiser. He left Brakeley to form his own capital campaign consulting firm, Development Management Associates, Inc. (DMA) and to earn his MBA at UCLA. Over fifteen years, he and partner Bob Zuer expanded DMA to $2 million in annual billings, serving clients throughout the Western United States, Great Britain and Australia.

0-595-20884-3